John
McGinley

Mission
Shaped
Living

Being
Witnesses
for Jesus
in Our
Everyday
Lives

DAVID **C** COOK

transforming lives together

MISSION SHAPED LIVING PARTICIPANT'S GUIDE
Published by David C Cook
4050 Lee Vance Drive
Colorado Springs, CO 80918 U.S.A.

Integrity Music Limited, a Division of David C Cook
Brighton, East Sussex BN1 2RE, England

The graphic circle C logo is a registered trademark of David C Cook.

The website addresses recommended throughout this book are offered as a
resource to you. These websites are not intended in any way to be or imply an
endorsement on the part of David C Cook, nor do we vouch for their content.

Details in some stories have been changed to protect
the identities of the persons involved.

All Scripture quotations are taken from Holy Bible, New International
Version® Anglicized, NIV® Copyright © 1979, 1984, 2011 by Biblica,
Inc.® Used by permission. All rights reserved worldwide.

ISBN 978-0-8307-8180-5
eISBN 978-0-8307-8182-9

© 2020 New Wine Resources, Ltd.

The Team: Ian Matthews, Liza Hoeksma, Jo Stockdale, Susan Murdock
Cover Design: Mark Prentice at beatroot.media
Cover Image: Josh Rose on Unsplash

Printed in the United Kingdom
First Edition 2020

1 2 3 4 5 6 7 8 9 10

061220

CONTENTS

Introduction

Go and make disciples of all nations, baptising them
in the name of the Father and of the Son and of the
Holy Spirit, and teaching them to obey everything
I have commanded you. And surely I am with you
always, to the very end of the age. (Matt. 28:19–20)

Welcome to Mission Shaped Living! We're really glad you and your small group are going to spend some time looking at how you can live as witnesses of Jesus Christ in your everyday lives.

Many of us find it hard to talk about mission; we want people to know God's love but we don't know how to share it with them. Mission Shaped Living (MSL) brings together some spiritual practices and principles that other ordinary Christians have found helpful, and gives you some steps to follow as you go on a journey of exploring how you can be the witness Jesus has called you to be for him. It's designed to equip us to live out our faith in Jesus in such a way that we lead others to follow him, just as Jesus said in his last words to his disciples (in Matt. 28 above). The focus of the course is on us being prayerful, joy-filled, thankful people who live our lives on mission with Jesus, knowing that he promised to give us his Holy Spirit to enable us to be his witnesses (Acts 1:8). We believe that if others are to come to trust in Jesus, it will come through the ordinary everyday witness of Christians in families, workplaces, gyms, coffee shops, schools, etc.—that's us.

AIM

The aim of this course is that we will grow closer to God and one another and we will be equipped with tools that enable us to share God's love and the good news of Jesus with others so that they can be saved.

STRUCTURE

There are eight sessions in MSL and each one is divided into three sections. Each of these is focused on one of the three relationships each Christian is called to: IN, UP, and OUT.

IN

Jesus said, 'A new command I give you: love one another. As I have loved you, so you must love one another. By this everyone will know that you are my disciples, if you love one another' (John 13:34–35). This is about our relationship with our Christian brothers and sisters.

Jesus has put us together in the family of the church so that we form a new community, filled with his love and witnessing to him through the ways that we love one another. The mission Jesus calls us to is never a solitary affair. How we build relationships of love, trust, vulnerability, and care through these sessions is as important as any faith sharing we engage in. And through being together we can encourage and challenge one another in our witness.

The core elements of each week that focus on IN are:

▶ How are you?

To foster this level of community, we will start each session with the question 'How are you?' This provides a good space to talk about how you are and how your week has been, as well as finding out about other people's lives so we can support one another.

▶ Testimony

Sharing stories from our own lives and testimonies of what God has done are powerful ways to understand and connect with one another, as well as to encourage one another about God's work. One Christian who is taking steps forward in faith can strengthen another through their story. It also helps us to learn together when things don't go the way we hoped, just as Jesus did with his disciples.

▶ Vision casting

Jesus constantly reminded his disciples that he and they were on a mission to reach others. It was there right at the beginning when he called them: 'Come, follow me … and I will send you out to fish for people' (Mark 1:17). The aim of this section is to keep reminding us we are being 'sent' by Jesus wherever we are.

▶ Accountability

> Jesus held his disciples to account for the lifestyle and practices he had called them to. We can talk in a group and have great hopes and plans, but we are all more likely to put things into practice when we know others will ask us how it went later. Healthy accountability involves each person sharing what they plan to do as a result of what they have studied and practised. We can support one another then celebrate and process our experiences together. (Accountability is not manipulative or overbearing pressure aimed at making people do what they don't want to do!)

UP

Jesus said, 'The most important [commandment] ... is this: "Hear, O Israel: the Lord our God, the Lord is one. Love the Lord your God with all your heart and with all your soul and with all your mind and with all your strength"' (Mark 12:29–30). This is about our relationship with God from which everything else flows, so in this section there will be times of worship, prayer, and engagement with a Bible passage.

Our life of mission is one of the responses we make to the love God has shown us in Jesus. Growing in our personal relationship with God and seeking the filling and leading of the Holy Spirit allows his presence in us to overflow to others (John 7:37–38), and this is at the heart of MSL.

OUT

Jesus said, 'The second [commandment] is this: "Love your neighbour as yourself"' (Mark 12:31). At the end of his ministry on earth, Jesus said, 'All authority in heaven and on earth has been given to me. Therefore go and make disciples of all nations' (Matt. 28:18–19).

Following Jesus involves being sent by him, loving others, and leading them to follow him, so each week we will finish the session with a very practical 'outward' action to ensure that what we've discussed doesn't just stay within our group but impacts others.

▶ Training

The best current equivalent of what the word 'disciple' meant in Jesus' day is an 'apprentice'—someone who is being trained on the job. We learn as we go along by practising the techniques of the more experienced person who is training us. This requires practising and failing, trying again, and improving. Most of us are uncomfortable with this to some degree—few people enjoy failing—but it is key to growth. We want to create a group where people feel safe to try new things and are encouraged that they can keep going no matter what the results.

▶ Activation

Once we have received training, we have to be intentional about putting it into practice, so a key part of each session is looking at putting the principle or tool discussed into action.

Gratitude

'Freely you have received; freely give' (Matt. 10:8).

We want gratitude to underpin all that we do. Being grateful has been identified as a key aspect of personal well-being, and being thankful for all that Jesus is and has done for us is also the key motivation for mission. We will regularly ask, 'What are you grateful for?' as a way of enabling one another to express gratitude and to give testimony.

The following diagram shows something of how all of this flows together and how the three relationships are held within our lives. Our outward mission flows from God's love in us and our shared love for one another.

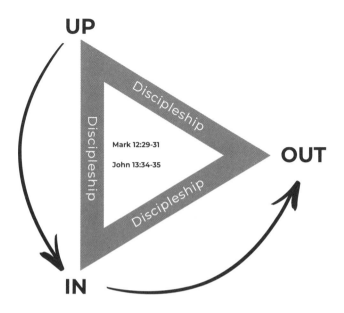

Personal Reflection

There are personal reflections each week in this Participant's Guide so that you have some resources to help you reflect on the session's theme before you meet again. These include:

> ▶ an encouraging story;
> ▶ a focus for prayer;
> ▶ another exercise to help you develop in that area.

We know you may be pushed for time so we've highlighted things that would be particularly helpful to focus on each week.

Being Sent

We are all starting in different places and so each of our journeys through the coming weeks will be unique. There is no expectation of us all starting at the same place or finishing in the same place at the end of our Mission Shaped Living journey, but we have all believed the good news of Jesus Christ and so each of us can take steps forward in our calling to be a witness for him. Like a baton in a relay race, we have received the gospel and we are now sent to pass it on.

Jesus called Peter, Andrew, James, and John to be his followers when they were fishermen. In Jewish culture the young men who showed most spiritual promise in the local synagogue were invited by a rabbi to be their disciple. All other young men were left to continue in their father's business. So from their vocation we know that these young men hadn't made the spiritual grade. Regardless, when they met Jesus, they were willing to follow him and learn from him, reminding us that following Jesus and being sent by him on mission is not about our ability; it is simply about being willing to become his apprentice, or a learner, which is all a disciple is.

IN

How are you?

How did you come to believe in Jesus?

What difference has he made to your life?

Vision Casting

Read:

Matthew 28:16–20
Acts 1:4–8

How do you feel about the fact that Jesus is calling you to represent him and reveal him to others?

Let's Get Practical: Recognising Our Missional Context

List the places and main relationships in which you spend the majority of your time each week:

Do you enter these places with a sense of being 'sent' by Jesus?

What are the challenges about being a witness for Jesus there?

UP

Prayer and Worship

Pray and bring all that we have been thinking and talking about to Jesus, thanking him for calling and choosing us to represent him, acknowledging our weaknesses and failures in this, and asking for his help.

Read Luke 10:1–20.

The sending of the seventy-two in this passage will form the basis of the structure of the rest of Mission Shaped Living.

Here is a brief summary of how each session title relates to this passage:

Confidence (vv. 2–3)

Courage (vv. 2–3)

Compassion (vv. 8–9)

Connecting (vv. 5–6)

Continuing (v. 7)

Conversion (v. 9)

OUT

Daily Prayer

Write a prayer to pray at the start of every day of the coming week; a prayer that offers yourself to God to be used to share his love and good news with others who you will meet that day.

Prayer of Consecration

Lord Jesus Christ, I am no longer my own but
yours.
In gratitude for your saving death on my behalf, I
offer my life to you afresh.
Call me to the mission of your kingdom and open
my eyes to the spiritual need of those
around me.

Give me your love and compassion for the lost, and
        strengthen me with your grace to serve
        them and be a blessing to them.
Send me in the power of your Holy Spirit to witness
        to the gospel and reveal you to those I
        meet.
Teach me how to make disciples and where I need to
        change my attitude, lifestyle, and habits.
I freely and wholeheartedly commit myself to this
        call, knowing that in everything you
        will give me your inspiration, strength,
        and grace.
Glorious and blessed God, Father, Son, and Holy
        Spirit, you are mine and I am yours. So
        be it.
Let this covenant now made on earth be fulfilled in
        heaven.
Amen.

SESSION 1: PERSONAL REFLECTION

An encouraging story:

> Edith was an eighty-two-year-old Parochial Church Council secretary in a rural Church of England parish. She attended an MSL group where she was asked to think of people around her who weren't yet Christians. She didn't think she knew anyone until people started to talk about her neighbours. She started to pray for the people who lived next door to her and opposite her. One day she saw the young man who lived next door walking with some difficulty past her front gate. She went outside and asked him what the problem was and he explained that he had developed a very painful skin condition. She invited him in for a cup of tea and after she had listened to his story she offered to pray with him. After she had prayed, he said how much better he felt. This was the first informal prayer Edith had ever prayed with someone.

A Focus for Prayer

Read John 20:19–23.

Take some time to reflect on the material from session 1, 'Being Sent'.

Connect with how you are feeling about Jesus calling you to share his love and good news with others. Don't try and hide from any feelings of fear or inadequacy—acknowledge them. Hopefully there might also be some positive feelings around God wanting to use you and you becoming aware that your life is significant to him.

Bring all of these to God in prayer and trust yourself to him.

Breathe: A Pattern of Daily Prayer

Have a look at the Breathe pattern of prayer shown below and think about your own daily pattern of prayer.

What works for you?

How might this pattern help you to grow in your relationship with God and in your mission?

Using the image of breathing we can create a rhythm of prayer each day that can help us to have deep points of connection with God. This helps us to keep closer to him throughout the day and in every situation.

Take a Deep Breath

If possible, at the beginning of each day, have a time of prayer and reading God's Word.

Pray for God to come close to you and fill you with his Spirit.

Read a passage of Scripture. As you read, ask questions about what God is revealing about himself and what he is saying to you about your life. Then respond and ask for God's help in living out what you've learnt.

Next, pray more widely for the needs of others and the world around us.

Finish by offering yourself to God using the prayer you have written, praying that he would give you an opportunity to show his love to others that day.

If you didn't have time in your group to write a prayer, the following points may help:

Offer yourself to God to be used and for opportunities to share his love with others.

Ask for God to help you and fill you with his Holy Spirit and give you his love for people.

Ask him to help you to see where he is at work.

Pray for him to prepare the hearts of those you will meet.

Ask him to give you an opportunity to show his love
to someone today.

Catch Your Breath

At different points in the day take time to pray and look around you
at the place you are in and the people who are around you, asking
God to bring his kingdom into that situation. You might want to set
yourself reminders to pray or to do it when you have a lunch break.
Ask God to help you see where he is at work.

Breathe Out

At the end of each day take time to reflect on the events of the day.
  Give thanks for all the signs of God's blessing and goodness.
  Repent of things you have got wrong.
  Reflect on where you shared God's love and who God is calling
you to.
  Trust to him the things you are anxious about.
  Ask God to bless you and minister to you as you sleep.

*How might this pattern of prayer connect with
the rhythm of your daily life? Think about when
and where you might pray each section.*

Vision for Salvation Exercise

The next exercise is to encourage you to have a real desire for and vision of someone you love coming to faith in Jesus.

 ▶ Think about someone you know who isn't a follower of Jesus (pick one person to start with).
 ▶ Imagine that it is now one year from today and you have led them to put their trust in Jesus.
 ▶ Pause and engage with what this looks like—perhaps they are now attending your small group or church services with you on Sundays.
 ▶ Imagine how this might have happened.

How do you feel?

What do you think you would have to do to enable that to happen?

What do you think might have to change for you to do this?

Journal

Journal

Confidence

In Luke's account of the calling of the first disciples, he records the miraculous catch of fish Jesus led Peter to experience. When Peter saw this, he fell at Jesus' feet and said, "'Go away from me, Lord; I am a sinful man!" … Jesus said … "Don't be afraid; from now on you will fish for people'" (Luke 5:8–10).

It is easy to fall into the danger of seeing mission and witness as *a set of practices to do* instead of *a life to live* in response to us encountering Jesus. This session is designed to bring us back to a place of remembering who Jesus is and responding to his call to share his love with others.

Jesus is the life-giver. He describes himself as 'the way and the truth and the life' (John 14:6), 'the resurrection and the life' (John 11:25), 'the bread of life' (John 6:25–59), and says that his followers would know 'fullness of life' (see John 10:10). Staying close to him allows his life to overflow from us, and remembering Jesus and being thankful for all that he is and has done for us personally releases joy in our lives. It is this that will allow our witness to be an overflow of our love for God and not just another thing on our to-do list.

Gratitude frees us to be generous and keeps alive our desire to share Jesus with others, so let's start the session this week by talking about what we're grateful for.

IN

How are you?

How did you get on praying the prayer that you wrote?

Did you notice a difference?

Have you got a story of God answering prayer this week or of being missional in any way?

Vision Casting

Why is Jesus' 'good news' worth sharing?

Thinking about what Jesus has done for you, what are you most grateful for today?

UP

Prayer and Worship

In a time of worship, take a few moments to remember Jesus' saving work on the cross and all that he has done in your lives, and to thank him for it.

Read John 4:1–26; 39–42.

What do we learn from Jesus' example of sharing his good news?

What difference does encountering Jesus make to this woman?

What is your response to this passage?

OUT

One of the striking things from Jesus' example was that he took time to sit and talk with the Samaritan woman and then stayed in her village for two days. Jesus had a reputation for 'eating with the sinners and tax collectors' (Mark 2:16). While he is sitting with her, he is listening to what the Holy Spirit is revealing about her and he then responds to this in how he speaks. Praying for someone while we are with them and asking God to lead us and show us anything he wants us to understand about that person is one of the ways that witnessing stops being done 'to' someone and becomes something we do 'with' Jesus, who loves this person so much.

Let's Get Practical: Listening to God

We're going to spend some time listening to God for each other. There is no pressure—just have a go and trust that God is prompting your thoughts and leading you.

Get together in pairs and sit in silence together for two minutes. While you do this in your heart ask God two questions:

1. What specifically do you love about this person?

2. What encouragement do you want me to bring them?

God's answers could come in a feeling, an image in our imagination, a Bible verse, or simply a phrase or line of thought.

Sharing Life with Others

The other part of Jesus' example is that he spent time with people and shared food with them. In your life at the moment who do you spend time with socially who isn't a Christian?

Jesus instructs the seventy-two disciples sent out on mission to stay in a home and eat the food served to them. Why can sharing a coffee or a meal with someone be a very personal experience?

In the coming week could you arrange to meet up with someone for a coffee or invite them round for a meal? Don't do it with an agenda other than seeking to love and bless that person. While you are with them, pray silently for God's blessing on them and ask if there is anything God wants you to understand about them or share with them.

Take some time to think, pray, and plan about who you could do this with, then share it with another member of the group and pray together.

SESSION 2: PERSONAL REFLECTION

An encouraging story:

> James was walking through a park one day, taking time to quietly pray for God's blessing on anyone he walked past. He noticed a man sitting on a bench and a thought came into his mind: 'Tell him that he will see his children again.' James had learned that this kind of thought was often from God but he was still nervous as he said this to the man: 'I'm a Christian and I am walking around the park praying to God. When I saw you, I thought that God might be giving me a message to say to you, which is that you will see your children again. Does that make sense?' The man began to cry. It turned out that his relationship with his wife had just ended and she had taken their children back to Poland. James was able to show how God loved him and cared about his loss, and he prayed for the man and invited him to church.

A Focus for Prayer

Read John 7:37–39.

A life of mission is an overflow of God's love and Spirit within you, or as Jesus describes it, 'Rivers of living water … [flowing] from

within them' (John 7:38). If this is the case then being full of the
Holy Spirit is key to a daily life of mission.

When have you felt most excited by Jesus and his presence in your life?

*What clues does that give you as to how you can keep your faith alive
day by day?*

*Take some time to pray for personal renewal and an openness to the
leading of the Holy Spirit.*

Asking God Questions Exercise

If we are going to grow in confidence in discerning God's voice, we have to learn to listen to him. One of the key factors in this is asking God questions and then waiting to see how he answers. You can ask him all kinds of questions, including:

- what he loves about a person or your town or city;
- how to solve a tricky problem at work;
- how he wants you to pray for the place where you work;
- how to be a good parent to your child;
- what he wants you to do next in leading someone to faith.

As soon as you pray and ask him a question, begin to listen. Spiritual listening involves becoming aware of any thought or image that comes to mind, or an emotion we start to feel that we didn't expect. God's answer may come through something someone else says, through creation, or even by a song we hear or something we see on TV. God is really creative when he wants to tell us something!

Once we think we have heard something, we have to decide if it is from God and, if it is, how he wants us to respond. Here is a helpful checklist of how to test if it is God speaking:

▶ Is it *consistent* with Scripture? God would never contradict what he has said in his written Word.

▶ The *character* of Jesus—does the idea 'feel' like Jesus in its heart and intent?

▶ *Consequence*—what would be the result of acting on the impression you have? Would it glorify Jesus and produce an outcome that would further God's kingdom?

▶ *Conviction* of the Spirit—did you pray for this and did you feel a sense of God's peace or presence when you sensed this message?

▶ *Counsel* of the saints—what do wise friends have to say?

Journal

Journal

Courage

In Luke 10, when Jesus sent the seventy-two out on mission, he sent them ahead to specific villages where he was planning to go. These villages are the equivalent of the workplaces, sports teams, colleges, families, etc. that Jesus is sending us to as his representatives. He knew that his disciples would need courage, which is why he warned them that they were being sent out 'like lambs among wolves' (v. 3). He didn't want them turning back when it became challenging, so he prepared them for it. Like them, we need to be prepared for the fact that leading others to follow Jesus will not be easy, but we are sent by him and he goes with us by his Holy Spirit who gives us courage.

IN

How are you?

How did you get on meeting up with someone and seeking to listen to God and bless them?

Are you finding time to pray your prayer every morning? How's that going?

What are you grateful for?

What's your experience been of sharing faith with non-Christians in the past?

What are the things that give you confidence in the gospel and in sharing your faith?

What are the things that reduce your confidence? Tick any below that are relevant to you and/or add your own.

- I don't know how to start conversations about faith.
- I worry about being rejected.
- I think that I won't be able to answer difficult questions.
- I am worried about spoiling a friendship.
- I don't want to come across as one of those judgmental/ crass Christians.

- I don't know how to make the Christian faith relevant to people.
- I don't have any close friendships/contact with people who aren't Christians.
- Other.

UP

Prayer and Worship

God's solution to the first disciples' fear and lack of confidence was to promise them he would be with them and fill them with the Holy Spirit. When he did this on the day of Pentecost, they moved from hiding away in a room together to spilling out onto the streets of Jerusalem and telling the good news of Jesus to everyone around them.

Read Acts 2:1–13 and John 16:7–15.

What does this teach us about God's Spirit and what he will do?

What does this teach me about how to live in relationship with the Holy Spirit?

Let's pray and ask God to empower us with his Holy Spirit.

OUT

Let's Get Practical: Mapping Your Relational World

Jesus sent the seventy-two in pairs to various villages, and Mission Shaped Living is based on the premise that wherever we are today

Jesus has commissioned us to reach those people. Our families and colleagues are our 'villages' so we have to ask, 'Who have I been sent to?'

Draw a circle at the centre of a page and write your name in it. Then draw circles round it, writing the names of the people you know and love who are far from God. Use the circles around their names to add people you know and who you share a relationship with. You now have the names of people to pray for.

Choose the names of five people who you have regular contact with, who you could witness to, and who you want to pray for to come to faith in Jesus.

1.
2.
3.
4.
5.

Pray for them every day to come to faith. You can pray for them all every day or simply name each of them before God and then pray for one person in depth each day; for example, Dave on Monday, Sarah on Tuesday, etc. You might find it helpful to put this list somewhere you see every day, along with the prayer offering yourself to God that you are praying; for example, in the book/ Bible you're reading, as the background on your phone, or on your bathroom mirror.

How Should I Pray for Them?

The Archbishop of York simply prays the Lord's Prayer over each of his five friends, or here is an example prayer which you can use:

> Heavenly Father, I thank you that you love X and that you long for them to know you. I pray for them in the name of Jesus Christ that you would pour out your Holy Spirit upon them and convict them of their sin and reveal Jesus to them. I ask you to stir up a spiritual hunger within them and take the blindness from their eyes. I pray that you would bless my friendship with them and that you would use me to draw them closer to you. Please show me your heart for them and what you are asking me to do as your ambassador. Direct their steps so that they come into contact with other Christians and speak to them through the circumstances of their life. I pray that they would come to faith in Jesus. Amen.

Take some time to write your own prayer.

Pray together in pairs for your five people and then commit to checking in during the week with your prayer partner to see how they are getting on every day—via text, WhatsApp, or phone call.

SESSION 3: PERSONAL REFLECTION

An encouraging story:

Stephen started to pray for five people he knew who didn't yet know Jesus. Two of those people were his brother and sister-in-law. A week after he had started to pray for them, he happened to be in the car with his sister-in-law on a family outing. She turned to him and said, 'I realise that I don't know anything about what you do in the church you go to. Could you tell me what happens in church?'

Stephen was amazed because in ten years of her being married to his brother neither of them had ever asked anything about faith or church. Now, a week after he had started to pray for them, she had asked him to talk about this. He realised God was hearing and answering his prayers.

A Focus for Prayer

Read John 1:35–42.

Andrew isn't well known or famous among the twelve apostles, but he does two really important things. Firstly, he follows Jesus himself, and then he invites his brother Simon Peter.

Take some time to remember the key people who God used to bring you to faith. What were the things they did that were significant in you coming to faith?

Pray that you would be able to be that person for the five people you have chosen to pray for.

Mission Styles Exercise

The student mission agency Fusion describes how each of us has a different natural 'mission style'. We may be one of the following people:

▶ A 'convince me' person.
   A 'convince me' person likes to weigh stuff up before coming to conclusions. They are thought-through, they know why they believe what they believe, and if they have questions they do their homework to find out more about Jesus.

▶ A 'show me' person.

A 'show me' person is practical and down-to-earth. They know God's love has to be shown through actions. They know what is required to get the job done and serve and love others alongside sharing what Jesus has done for them.

▶ A 'talk with me' person.

A 'talk with me' person loves to connect through conversation. They really enjoy sharing deeply with someone else, especially when they get the chance to bring Jesus into the story.

▶ A 'let me experience' person.

A 'let me experience' person just goes ahead and tries stuff. They trust their instincts and have a go at sharing Jesus in new ways and with new people, even if they're not sure how it'll work out.

Which one do you think you are? If you're not sure, you could take Fusion's quick online test at https://missionstyles.org. Understanding yourself will help you to see why some of the exercises and practices in MSL will feel easier and others harder. And it will help you to understand how you will naturally be able to be involved in God's mission.

Journal

Journal

Compassion

The compassion of Jesus was described by the gospel writers on a number of occasions. The apostle Paul writes: 'Praise be to the God and Father of our Lord Jesus Christ, the Father of compassion and the God of all comfort, who comforts us in all our troubles, so that we can comfort those in any trouble with the comfort we ourselves receive from God' (2 Cor. 1:3–4).

This reminds us that our call to be witnesses for Jesus comes within a wider call, which is to share the compassionate love God has for people. The work of evangelism has been summarised as three actions: prayer, care, and share. We have looked at prayer and now we will look at how caring for others can demonstrate God's love. Our desire to share Jesus with people comes from our love for them because their greatest need is for salvation.

IN

How are you?

How did you get on praying for five people each day?

Are there signs of God answering your prayers in any way?

Are there any other stories of God using you in mission?

Vision Casting

Read 2 Corinthians 5:14–21.

The work of mission is a ministry of love and compassion. Paul says that his work comes from Christ's love motivating him, and he then presents it as a work of reconciliation—us being used to repair the broken relationship between people and God. We can do this because we have come to know God's love for us. We are brand-new people and each of us has a story to tell of how Jesus has transformed our lives. He calls us as ambassadors of Christ; this is why what we are talking about is so important.

Write your name in your workbook above the following title:

An Ambassador of Jesus Christ

What does an ambassador do?

What does this communicate about our role on behalf of God's kingdom in this world?

Imagine you are introducing yourself in this way: '_____. An Ambassador of Jesus Christ.' No matter what else we might say about ourselves in our different roles, this is what the Bible says our title is.

UP

Prayer and Worship

Read Luke 15:1–10.

What does this teach us about:

God and how he feels towards people who don't know him? (His desire, value, and compassion for people who are lost.)

His active response in looking for those who are lost?

How do you need to respond?

Have a time of prayer in which you ask God to give you his heart for the people he has sent us to.

OUT

In Luke 10, Jesus talks about healing those who are sick. He didn't just speak about the kingdom; he showed God's love in action. Our sharing of Jesus with others must come from a genuine love for them.

What do you know about the five people you have started to pray for? Do you know how they take their coffee or tea? What about their families? How much do you know about their lives before you came to know them? What do they care about and love to do?

Pick one of your people and write down everything you know about them and their lives, including what needs they have that you could help meet in order to show God's love to them.

Let's Get Practical: Text a Friend

We are going to show our care for one of the five people we are
praying for by texting them. You can say you were thinking of
them and would love to do X for them as a way of supporting
them. Or you can say that you were thinking of them and wondering how they are and ask if there is anything particularly you
could pray for them. Choose which person to text and then pray
in pairs for God to prepare their hearts to receive the text. Then
send the message!

Praying with a Non-Christian

*Have you ever prayed with someone outside of a church context?
How did it go? This doesn't need to be a 'success' story to be something you share!*

When someone shares a need, you can say that you will be praying for them—but what about offering to pray with someone in that moment? Why do you think this can be important?

We are going to practise praying for one another to help us get used to it, so it doesn't feel so alien to offer it to a friend outside of church.

Some simple steps:

- Ask for permission—can I pray for you? (If they say yes, say, 'Can I pray with you now?' If they say no, consider how you could move the conversation on so they don't feel awkward.)
- Pray very short prayers, using nonreligious language.
- Use the name of Jesus as a way of ensuring people know this is Christian prayer.
- Pray with your eyes open so it looks like a natural conversation.
- If you want to lay a hand on them, place it gently on their shoulder. (It's a good idea to ask them if they're okay with that first.)

- If you are praying for physical healing, command healing of the ailment in the way Jesus did. (Remember that you have authority and you don't need to shout!)

A simple prayer might be:

Father God, thank you that you love X and that you
care about *(the problem)*.
Please *(whatever they have asked for)* and send your
Holy Spirit to do this.
And please be close to them and let them know your
love and peace.
In Jesus' name. Amen.

Break into pairs and choose a genuine need your partner can pray for. Take it in turns to role-play, sharing that need, the other person offering to pray, and then praying.

To finish, pray together as a group for an opportunity to pray with someone this week.

SESSION 4: PERSONAL REFLECTION

An encouraging story:

Sarah works as an administrator in an office and is a mum to two children. When she attended the Mission Shaped Living course, she said she could never do anything that involved praying for others or talking about her faith because she lacked confidence. Her group decided to practise praying for one another each week and to set the challenge that whenever they heard someone express a need they would offer to pray.

One day Sarah's colleague Julie was telling her how depressed she was because of some personal health and family issues. Before she could stop herself, Sarah said, 'Could I pray with you?' Julie said yes and Sarah then prayed a simple prayer affirming that God loved Julie and asking him to help her and heal her. At the end of the prayer Sarah wanted to run away and hide because of her embarrassment but Julie was clearly emotional and thanked Sarah. She then said that for the past three months she had started to pray because she was so desperate about her situation and wondered if God was even there. Now that Sarah had prayed with her, she knew he

was. Sarah and Julie arranged to meet each week for
lunch to talk about faith.

Do you believe that God could release his blessing or healing
through you to someone else? What we believe about ourselves really
matters as it will determine what we will be willing to do on mission
with Jesus!

A Focus for Prayer

Read 1 Corinthians 13:1–8.

Here are three simple questions about love:

*Do you love God? (Reflect on whether your heart towards God is full
of love and gratitude and a desire to serve him.)*

*Do you love the people around you? (How is this shown in your
daily life?)*

Do you love helping people connect with God? (What shapes your answer to this question?)

Making Plans Exercise

This week plan to do one of the three missional practices you looked at in the group session on 'Compassion'. Think about who and how you might seek to bless, serve, or pray for someone, especially one of the five people you have been praying for because God will already be at work in them. Make a plan about what you will do and perhaps share it by text with other members of the group so they can pray for you.

Journal

Journal

Session 5

Connecting

Being a witness for Jesus involves speaking for him, having conversations about faith with people, asking questions, and telling stories. When Jesus was preparing the seventy-two disciples to go out, he talked them through the different reactions that people will have. The really good news from Luke 10:1–20 is that Jesus says we only have to stay and share with people who are open to this. Because the passage describes the disciples bringing a blessing of 'peace to this house' and people receiving this peace (vv. 5–6), we can call these receptive people a 'person of peace' or more simply a 'God-prepared person'.

The problem is that we don't know how people will respond before we start to share with them and whether they are a person of peace. So this session is designed to help us think about how we can 'connect' with people spiritually in a simple way that is our equivalent of saying 'peace be upon you.' When we have done this, we can see whether they are open to us taking the conversation further and beginning a journey of faith with them. Isn't it liberating to remember we don't have to keep sharing the gospel with people who don't welcome it!

IN

How are you?

Have you had a reply to your text from the last session?

How did you get on taking the opportunity to bless, serve, or pray for someone?

Vision Casting

What is your favourite rescue story from a book or film?

Why do we find these inspiring?

Read Luke 15:1–7.

UP

Prayer and Worship

Looking for God-prepared people: pray for five, find the one.

Read Luke 10:1–11.

There are different responses to us sharing God's love with people. Some receive it and some reject it, but the good news is that Jesus says we only have to stay and share with people who are open.

Because the passage describes the peace of God staying on people who are ready to receive Jesus, we can call these people a 'person of peace' or more simply a 'God-prepared person'.

This strategy of Jesus is really helpful. It can be summarised as:

▶ speak a blessing of peace on someone;
▶ if they reject it, walk away;
▶ if they accept it, stay with them.

Here is a list of what saying 'peace be on this house' can look like today. We call this 'asking questions and telling stories'.

- Ask them questions about where they are spiritually. For example:

Can I pray for you?

Do you feel close or far away from God?

What has been your spiritual experience in the past?

- Invite them to a Christian event such as a Sunday service, an Alpha Course, a missional community, etc.
- Tell stories of what God has done in your life.
- Tell the gospel story.

Do you know if any of the five people you are praying for are 'God-prepared people'?

How do you know?

OUT

Let's Get Practical: Telling Your Story

Jesus continually asked questions and told stories. We will look at different aspects of this in the coming weeks, but today we will look at 'telling your story'.

> The man from whom the demons had gone out begged to go with him, but Jesus sent him away, saying, 'Return home and tell how much God has

done for you.' So the man went away and told
all over town how much Jesus had done for him.
(Luke 8:38–39)

Sharing your story can help family, friends, and people you
meet understand the difference Jesus has made to your life and that
he can do the same for them. It can be your 'big' story of coming
to faith but also a testimony of what God has done in your life
recently.

The best way to be ready to do this is to practise telling your
story in three simple sections:

1. What your life was like before you encountered Jesus.
2. How you encountered Jesus.
3. How your life has changed since.

Guidance on telling your story:

▶ Keep it simple—don't include lots of unnecessary
detail.
▶ Keep it focused on Jesus and not just on you.
▶ Avoid religious jargon that people won't understand.
▶ Be honest—real stories connect with people, so tell the
truth about yourself.
▶ Keep it short—ideally less than two minutes.

Make notes in the following three sections, and then break into pairs to practise telling your story in no more than two minutes.

Section 1:
Begin with the phrase, 'There was a time in my life when …'
Explain a time when you didn't follow Jesus, or if you have been brought up as a Christian, when your faith was not as personal or alive as it is now.

Section 2:
'Then …'
Explain how you came to faith in Jesus, or how your faith came alive.

Section 3:

'And now ...'

Explain the difference Jesus has made to your life.

Keep practising your story at every opportunity—while you're driving home, when you're in the shower, etc.

Who could you tell your story to in the coming week? It might be one of the five people you are praying for. You could say, 'I'm in a Christian group that meets each week and they have asked me to share how I became a Christian with someone outside the group to see what they think about it—could I do it with you?' Or you could say to a long-term friend, 'I realise that we have been friends for some time and I have never explained how I became a Christian—could I share that with you?'

SESSION 5: PERSONAL REFLECTION

An encouraging story:

Norman and Richard were neighbours who had exchanged 'good mornings' every day for about seven years as Richard headed off to work. One day it suddenly dawned on Richard that he didn't even know his neighbour's name, so he stopped and asked him. For the next few weeks they started saying, 'Morning, Norman,' and 'Morning, Richard,' and Richard said it felt good to know his name! Richard was sitting in the local coffee shop one morning when he saw Norman going by, so he knocked on the window and invited him for coffee; it was easy because he now knew his name! They had a chat for a good hour; Norman told Richard all about his life, how his wife had passed away, and of his love of steam trains. Richard reflected how it was good to get to know him after all this time.

The weeks went by and it was coming up to Christmas. Richard was shopping with his daughter and spotted a DVD and book collection of the greatest British steam railways. 'Norman would like that,' he thought, so he bought it and wrapped it up. A few days before Christmas, they exchanged good mornings and Richard gave Norman his present. Norman was slightly taken aback and wanted to know why he had bought him a present. Richard explained that he was a Christian and that Christmas meant a lot to him, that giving gifts was a symbol of the gift that we get in the birth of Jesus, and that he hoped Norman would enjoy his gift. Richard didn't see Norman for a couple of weeks, but when he bumped into him in the village, he asked him if he had time for coffee. Norman said he didn't because he was off to a Bible study. 'I hadn't realised you went to church,' Richard said. 'I didn't,' Norman replied. 'Not until you gave me your gift. I've been going since Christmas as someone invited me.'

It's funny what can happen when you ask someone their name!

A Focus for Prayer

Read John 9:1–12.

In this passage the blind man simply tells his experience of the healing Jesus brought to his life, and when he was asked a question he didn't know, he simply said, 'I don't know.'

As you remember your story of coming to faith, try to imagine what life would be like if Jesus hadn't led you to follow him. Think about what it might be like to live without knowing his love. Think about answers to prayer that you have had and the purpose Jesus has given you. Remember the difference that the hope of eternal life gives you.

Give thanks for this and pray for those who you love who don't know this same hope.

Understanding how your story connects

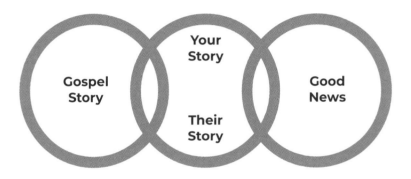

The power of your story is how it helps people to understand that the gospel story is good news for them. That happens when you are able to describe how the gospel story became good news for you in a way that connects with their lives, perhaps by you telling the story of how you came to faith or by telling a smaller story. For example, if your friend talks about parenting troubles you could talk about the difference being able to pray for your children has made to your life and then offer to pray for them. Or if your friend talks about mental health problems, you can share your own struggles with this and how knowing God's love makes such a difference.

Take some time to think about your five people and how your life and their lives connect, and some smaller stories that might be interesting for them to hear. Pray for an opportunity to share these with them.

Journal

Journal

Continuing

Jesus' instruction to the seventy-two was that when their blessing of peace was received they were to stay in the home where they were welcomed. They were to eat the food offered, declare that God's kingdom was coming to the household, and heal the sick. Jesus was explaining his strategy. We are to keep searching for and blessing people until we find one who is ready to receive him. Then we stay with them and help them in their journey of coming to faith in him. This requires spiritual discernment and lots of practical steps, persistent prayer, and patience. Jesus is the good shepherd who knows how to lead people back to the Father. We need to learn what our part in that journey is.

IN

How are you?

Is anyone grateful for something from the past week?

How did you get on sharing your story with someone?

Do you have any other stories to share?

Practise telling your story to a new person in the group.

Vision Casting

Jesus said, 'Come, follow me … and I will send you out to fish for people' (Mark 1:17).

The next step in mission is 'continuing'. In Luke 10, Jesus tells the seventy-two that when they have found their 'person of peace' they should stay with them and share food with them. The work of evangelism is a long-term process that involves sharing our lives with people and helping them to take steps towards faith in Jesus. We can think of it like stepping-stones across a stream. We are offering ourselves to God to help encourage our 'person of peace' to take another step forward.

When someone responds positively to our steps to bless them, and we discover their openness to God, we know they are a person of peace. We now have to 'stay' with them and help them take the next step.

UP

Prayer and Worship

Read Psalm 34:1–10.

What aspect of God's goodness are you most thankful for today?

Read Luke 19:1–10.

Jesus was renowned for attending meals and parties with people who weren't law-abiding Jews. Jesus shared a meal with Zacchaeus. Why do you think he did that?

What do you think Zacchaeus and Jesus talked about that could have made such a dramatic impact on him?

What can we learn from Jesus' example?

The key to 'staying' with your person of peace is regular time with them in which you share life and enjoy a deep friendship. This may be doing fun things together, but also talking about life (its joys and struggles) and talking spiritually, inviting them to actively pursue faith on an Alpha Course or by reading the Bible alone or with you (we will talk some more about this next week).

Have you ever invited a friend to a church event/evangelistic course? How did that go?

What helps people to be ready to accept such invitations?

What do you understand by the phrase 'Don't say people's "nos" for them'?

Why can we be tempted to do this?

OUT

Thinking Strategically

Take some time to each pray over one or two names on your list and ask God to show you what he is leading you to do next. It may not be a great revelation; it may simply be common sense, such as 'I haven't met up with them recently so I'll give them a call and arrange to see them.' Or it might be an idea to lend them a book or send them a link to an appropriate talk on YouTube. It could be baking them a cake or offering to babysit for their children. Or it could be time to invite them to a church service or Alpha Course.

When we love people, we act intentionally to show our care for them. The way we show our desire to help someone to come to faith in Jesus is to reflect on where they are on this journey and to pray 'What can I do next, Lord?' You're asking God to guide you in what you can do proactively to encourage them on their journey of faith. People's journey to faith in Jesus is always personal and unique and so your job is not to force them through a process but to intuitively sense what the next thing is that you could do to help them. Sometimes it is simply to wait and love them; sometimes it is right to bring a clear challenge to them to take the next step of faith. How do we know? We ask God.

Let's Get Practical: Taking the Initiative

To give us a shared experience of being proactive and intentional, today we are going to each contact one of our five people while we're together. (It may be the same person as a couple of sessions ago or a different one.) Try one of the following messages if it's suitable:

▶ Text with the invitation to meet or the offer of help you sensed God prompt you to make when we prayed earlier.

▶ Ask them if they would like to meet up and suggest how to do this. For example, would you like to come to supper in the next week, would you like to meet for a coffee, etc.

▶ Say that you were thinking of them and wondering
   how they are and if there is anything you could pray
   for them specifically.

This may feel risky and awkward, but we want to learn and grow
in this together. When we step across social boundaries and intro-
duce spirituality into our friendship, it can be difficult but it can
open people up to God so it's worth the risk!

SESSION 6: PERSONAL REFLECTION

An encouraging story:

Emma is a mum of young boys and a part-time GP. She felt challenged on her Mission Shaped Living course to invite friends to the next Alpha Course. She listed eight people and made a plan to invite them. They all said 'no'. But what she realised were some important things that often hold us back from inviting people:

- They were happy and relaxed to be invited.
- They assumed that it was a good thing they were being invited to.
- They felt bad about not accepting the invitation (instead of her worrying that they would be offended by the invitation, it was they who were worried that they were offending her).
- Some would have come if they had been able and said 'please ask me again'.
- It didn't negatively affect any of her friendships.

Emma said that fear had held her back before, but nothing she was afraid of actually happened. She described how her faith grew as she prayed

before each invitation and she felt joyful in obeying
God and being known by her friends as a Christian.

A Focus for Prayer

Read Matthew 9:9–13.

Matthew starts to follow Jesus and then invites his friends to
a meal so that they can meet him too. We can only imagine how
nervous Matthew felt about how it would go. Ask God to give you
an idea of what you could invite one of your friends to in order to
help them meet Jesus. A special service at church? An Alpha Course
(or equivalent)? A meal at your house with your friends from church?
Use the next exercise to work out who to invite and what to do next.

Spiritual Assessment Exercise

Write the names of your five people in the space below.

Using arrows, indicate any sense of movement or signs that God
is at work in them.

↑ An upward arrow means they are showing signs of opening up
to God.

↓ A downward arrow reflects that they have reacted negatively to something spiritual that you did or they have stepped back from spiritual engagement.

← A horizontal arrow means no change.

The key, particularly for people who have responded positively, is to ask God 'what next?' (i.e., what could you do next to help this person come closer to God?).

What insights does this give you about your friends and what to do next in helping them to come to faith? Using the analogy of a traffic light, is it:

- ▶ green for go—you can see a next step and sense God calling you to take it;
- ▶ orange for wait and get ready—keep praying with some fresh understanding of what to pray for;
- ▶ red for stop—they are rejecting any engagement with the Christian faith and you can pray about barriers being broken down.

Spend some time praying for your friends in light of this.

Journal

Journal

Conversion

The key thing we want to look at in this session is: If your friend was ready to come to faith, would you know how to explain the gospel simply and help them surrender their lives to Christ?

IN

How are you?

How did it go with the invitation to meet up with your friends and the response to the text?

Any other testimonies of living missionally?

Vision Casting

What was the process of coming to faith like for you?

How long from when you first heard about Jesus did it take to come to a place where you knew you were following him?

Was there a clear moment or was it a process?

What were the key factors in you coming to faith?

There are many ways that people come to faith and this is the work of the Holy Spirit, but here are the most common things that help people come to that point:

- ▶ One-to-one conversation and prayer with a Christian friend.
- ▶ Through attending an Alpha Course.
- ▶ Attending an evangelistic event with a clear call to faith.
- ▶ Through becoming a regular attendee at Sunday services or being involved in a missional community or

small group, which gradually leads to a point where they decide to follow Christ.

(Often it is a combination of the above.)

UP

Prayer and Worship

Read Psalm 40:1–10.

Listen to the psalm and look for a verse that connects with you. Prepare a prayer that flows from that verse—perhaps thanking God for saving you or a prayer for God's help to speak about him.

The key to people coming to faith is for them to begin consistently engaging with faith and God in one of the ways listed above. You can help your friend to come to faith by meeting up and reading gospel stories about Jesus together. We deliberately keep the Bible study sections in Mission Shaped Living simple because we hope that when you come to read a gospel passage with a 'person of peace' you can follow the same simple process of questions.

A reminder of the three kinds of questions we have been following in our Bible studies:

What does this tell me about Jesus (and therefore God because Jesus is God)?

What does this tell me about people and human life?

How do we need to respond to this?

These questions are not restrictive and they shouldn't limit you from following up with other questions as you discuss and talk about a passage.

We recommend the following passages—which we call the Seven Stories of Hope—for people who are developing an interest in faith:

- ▶ The woman who wept at Jesus' feet: Luke 7:36–50.
- ▶ Accepted by God: Luke 18:9–17.
- ▶ A hole in the roof: Luke 5:17–26.
- ▶ Two lost sons: Luke 15:11–32.
- ▶ Death and forgiveness: Mark 15:16–39.
- ▶ New life, new purpose: Matthew 28:1–20.

▶ Which soil are you?: Mark 4:1–20.

OUT

The Three Circles

A key part of the process of coming to faith is understanding what Jesus has done for us and how his death relates to our need for God. We have to be able to explain the gospel in an understandable way, so we're going to look at a tool called 'The Three Circles'. It is simple to learn and is helpful as it starts with things people understand (the good in the world and also our shared experience of pain and brokenness) as well as addressing the issue of sin.

While drawing the diagram for someone, you could say something like the following:

We live in a broken world. When we look around, or watch the news, we see messed-up stuff everywhere. Awful things happen to people: murder, theft, depression, the suffering caused by war, famine, and cancer. If we're honest, we all have an experience of that brokenness—some of that will be the pain caused to us by things like a relationship breakup, illness, financial pressures, or addiction.

For me I have had (add your examples).

Then there are things that we have done that have caused others pain. There have been loads of things that I've done that I regret, including (add your examples).

I'm sure you can think of some for yourself too. When we see brokenness in this world, it can often make us think that there can't be a God who loves us.

But alongside the pain we also see goodness and beauty. It might be the miracle of a child being born, the love we share with someone, how moved we are by a piece of music, the courage of someone overcoming their pain with such grace, the beauty of a sunrise, or the intricacy with which science shows this world is designed. There are definitely many amazing things in this world! That's because we can still see the evidence of God's design for this world; when he made it, it was good, and the plan was that we would live with him in this world forever.

How do we hold together the two realities of pain and brokenness in the world and God's love for us? The way Christians understand it is that God created this world for good and for us to know his love, but we thought we knew a better way than his design and turned our backs on him; we rejected God's plan and love for us. We call this selfishness and rejection of God 'sin'.

So we find ourselves in the midst of sin and brokenness; often we want to get out of it, but we can't. We try all sorts of things to 'fix' that sense of brokenness: we try to numb the pain with alcohol or buying things to make ourselves feel better; we try to earn loads of money or succeed academically; we seek a new relationship in the hope that it will make the pain go away. We can even try attending church or following a religion. Each of these things is like a bungee cord and, though we get a little further away from our sin and brokenness, we soon get pulled back into it again and we are left with a sense of restlessness and lack of fulfillment.

There was a time in my life when (share your own story).

God knew we were in this mess and he didn't want to leave us like that, so he came in the form of his only Son, Jesus. He lived a perfect life and revealed God's love to us by loving people who were broken and rejected, healing the sick, and setting people free. He then allowed himself to be killed on a cross to pay for all our sin and brokenness, and then he came back to life in order to make a new kind of life possible for all of us. He said that if we turn and believe in him, putting our trust in him and following him with our lives, then we could be set free from our brokenness and sin. In him we cross over into new life where we discover God's love and good design for us.

That's what Jesus has done for me (share your own story).

Where do you think you are in this picture? Over here, on God's design, or are you over here, feeling a bit stuck in sin and brokenness?

Where would you like to be?

Is there anything that would stop you from turning and believing in Jesus now?

Take some time to practise drawing the diagram, first on your own and then in pairs.

Is there anyone you could share this with? If not a non-Christian, find a Christian in the week ahead to share this with as practice.

Take some time to thank Jesus for his gift of salvation and pray for a time when you could share this good news with your friends.

SESSION 7: PERSONAL REFLECTION

An encouraging story:

> Ruth is a student who was meeting another student for coffee after they attended an evangelistic event the night before. Her friend was clearly interested by what she had heard and as she asked questions Ruth suggested that she explain the Christian faith using The Three Circles diagram. She told her testimony as part of it. At the end of it, she asked her friend if she would like to put her faith in Jesus, and she did! Ruth said, 'It was because I had learned The Three Circles tool that I felt confident to have that conversation. I never thought I would be someone who Jesus could use to lead someone to salvation— I'm amazed!'

A Focus for Prayer

Read John 3:1–18.

Here Nicodemus meets up with Jesus one-to-one, and Jesus answers his questions and challenges him to be born again.

Reflecting on this passage and Ruth's story, do you think that you could lead someone to put their faith in Jesus?

What affects how you answer that question?

Take your reflection to God in prayer.

Stories of Hope Exercise

Why not take one of the other gospel passages from the Seven Stories of Hope? Try and remember the questions and practise engaging with the passage using them. Imagine leading one of your friends through it.

Journal

Journal

Mission Shaped Living

Peter writes, 'In your hearts revere Christ as Lord. Always be prepared to give an answer to everyone who asks you to give the reason for the hope that you have. But do this with gentleness and respect' (1 Pet. 3:15). This describes a life devoted to Jesus as Lord and an attitude of being ready to share that he is the one who gives us hope. The aim of Mission Shaped Living has been to give us practices and tools which will enable us to be ready to witness for Jesus in our everyday life. As we come to the end of the course, it will be important to plan how we can continue to grow in confidence in this lifestyle.

IN

How are you?

Did you use The Three Circles tool with someone?

What are you grateful for from this Mission Shaped Living journey?

What has been your biggest insight/step forward?

Vision Casting

Read Matthew 13:18–23.

Here Jesus tells a story about the miracle seed of the kingdom. The seed contains everything necessary to save and transform a person's life, but there is an issue with the soil the seed lands on—the state of the hearts and minds who hear the gospel. In Luke 10, Jesus talks about the harvest being plentiful, which is a picture of many people being prepared for the gospel and ready to be saved. But Jesus says there is a problem: there aren't enough labourers out in the fields.

UP

Prayer and Worship

Read Acts 2:1–12.

We are going to have a time where we acknowledge our need of the Holy Spirit to empower us in our witness.

Read Acts 2:38–47.

What did the early church reveal about God?

What aspects of the early church's life challenge you?

How do you need to respond to this passage?

What we have shared together on Mission Shaped Living has tried to reflect these values:

- ▶ Hearing the vision for mission each time we gathered.
- ▶ Sharing lives of vulnerability, testimony, and accountability.
- ▶ Being fuelled by prayer and the Holy Spirit.
- ▶ Staying committed to living out our faith and supporting one another to do this.

According to Matthew 28:18–20, we're to make disciples and teach them how to follow Jesus. If we're going to keep living mission-ally, we will need to keep these elements in our lives.

OUT

How could you do some mission work together? Here are four ideas of what you could plan to do:

1. Host a social event.

Have a low-key social event that would fit with a number of the five people that you have all been praying for. Plan it, pray for it, and then see how your friends respond to the invitation.

2. Offer to pray for people in your local community.

Together, go out into a central shopping area of your commu-nity or door to door in some streets in your neighbourhood. In pairs, approach someone or knock at a door and explain you are from a local church and that you want to bless people, and then ask, 'What could we pray for you?' If people aren't sure how to answer, you can ask, 'If God were to do a miracle for you, what would you ask him to do?' Then pray for them and see what God does. You could also ask, 'At this moment in your life, do you feel near or far from God?' and see where the conversation leads.

3. Treasure hunting.

Meet as a group, ready to go out onto the streets of your local area. Pray together and ask God to give you an understanding of people he wants you to share his love with. We call it 'treasure hunt-ing' because people are God's greatest treasure and the revelations given by the Spirit are like clues. Those clues may be that in prayer you see a person with a particular characteristic or type of clothing, for example, and God may give you understanding of what the person is going through (a sick relative, they've lost their job, etc.). Or God may give you a location to visit. Take these clues and prayerfully look to see how God guides you as you go. When you meet someone you feel God wants you to talk to, find a way of explaining that you were praying and felt God lead you to them because he loves them. If you offer a word and it doesn't mean anything to them, they won't mind, but if you find someone who God has prepared, then God's kingdom can come to that person in wonderful ways.

4. Host an evangelistic evening or course.

After all of your prayer and sharing with your five friends, why not plan an event to help people come to faith? It could be that you host a meal or coffee morning, with someone giving a testimony at the end with a presentation of The Three Circles and a prayer for salvation. Or you might want to run an Alpha Course in a home that you can invite everyone to.

Let's finish as we began by saying the prayer of consecration together:

Lord Jesus Christ, I am no longer my own but yours.
In gratitude for your saving death on my behalf, I
offer my life to you afresh.
Call me to the mission of your kingdom and open
my eyes to the spiritual need of those
around me.

Give me your love and compassion for the lost, and
strengthen me with your grace to serve
them and be a blessing to them.

Send me in the power of your Holy Spirit to witness
to the gospel and reveal you to those I
meet.

Teach me how to make disciples and where I need to
change my attitude, lifestyle, and habits.

I freely and wholeheartedly commit myself to this
call, knowing that in everything you
will give me your inspiration, strength,
and grace.

Glorious and blessed God, Father, Son, and Holy
Spirit, you are mine and I am yours. So
be it.

Let this covenant now made on earth be fulfilled in
heaven. Amen.

SESSION 8: PERSONAL REFLECTION

An encouraging story:

> Patrick had invited a friend from work, Scott, to the Alpha Course. Scott had a great time on Alpha and opened up spiritually, but he didn't come to faith. Patrick was disappointed and didn't know what to do next. He realised that he had been trained in how to read a 'Stories of Hope' gospel story with someone and felt prompted to ask Scott if he'd like to meet up once a month and read something from the Bible and discuss it (he was convinced that Scott would say no). Amazingly, Scott said yes and they started to do this, and Patrick discovered the way he could *continue* to walk with Scott towards faith in Jesus.

A Focus for Prayer

Read Acts 8:26–40.

After the formation of the church in Acts 2, God used so many different people and ways to spread the gospel. The key was each person being obedient to what God asked them to do next. Here in Acts 8, Philip obeys the angel's instructions to go south on the desert road, literally to the middle of nowhere. It makes no sense, but Philip obeys and the result is that the Ethiopian is converted and the gospel reaches Africa.

'What Next?' Exercise

For you to continue to live missionally, you simply have to regularly ask God, 'Lord, what next?' and listen for a prompt, a thought process, an idea—and then obey it.

You can ask 'what next?' for yourself. With the understanding of where you are in the process of making disciples, why not ask God to show you how you can take the next step to become confident in God using you in one of the missional practices you haven't tried yet.

Or you can ask 'what next?' for one of the people you are praying for—what is the next thing you can do to help them come closer to knowing Jesus?

Try it now. Choose your focus—your own discipleship or one of the people you are praying for. Pray an opening prayer to come before God, and centre yourself on him.

Ask, 'Lord, what next?' And capture whatever you sense God prompting you to think about. It won't necessarily be fully formed, but whatever it is, begin to think and pray about how to obey it.

Then choose to have *courage* and obey it.

Once you have done this, review it, talk about it with friends, notice what God is doing and what you're learning. Then ask, 'Lord, what next?' again.

The process of discipleship is simply taking the next step. God rarely gives us a long-term plan, but he is always ready to lead someone who is asking him what he is calling them to do next.

You're now set for life!

Journal

Journal

Resources for you and your Church from

DAVID ⓒ COOK

transforming lives together

A Call to Act

A practical tool for individual, churches, and small groups, and incorporating discussion questions and accompanying videos, A Call to Act demonstrates that, in order to engage with poverty and need, we must re-evaluate our own attitudes and adopt a poverty-busting lifestyle.

RELEASED: *SEPTEMBER 2020* **PRICE:** *£11.99* **ISBN:** *9780830780686*

500 Prayers for the Christian Year

Written in accessible 'non-Churchy' language, and with prayers based on the Bible readings for every Sunday of all three years of the Lectionary, plus all major Christian holidays.

RELEASED: *OCTOBER 2020* **PRICE:** *£11.99* **ISBN:** *9780830782468*

'40 Prayers' series

Designed to be affordable, accessible, and portable, each volume contains 40 prayers for use either during a specific season in the Christian calendar, key areas of resource for Churches, or for particular seasons of life.

40 PRAYERS FOR ADVENT *9780830782307*
40 PRAYERS FOR THE CHRISTMAS SEASON *9780830782314*
40 PRAYERS FOR ALL-AGE WORSHIP *9780830782321*
40 PRAYERS FOR YOUR QUIET TIME *9780830782338*

RELEASED: *OCTOBER 2020* **PRICE:** *£4.99*

Saints Alive!

Saints Alive! is a well-loved nine-week course, completed by hundreds of thousands of people worldwide, introducing people to faith in God through the power of the Holy Spirit, integrating into the life of the church and moving out into ministry in their everyday lives.

LEADER'S MANUAL: £8.99 *ISBN: 9780830781485*
PARTICIPANT'S JOURNAL: £9.99 *ISBN: 9780830781492*
DVD: £14.99 *ISBN: 9780830781508*
RELEASED: *OCTOBER 2020*

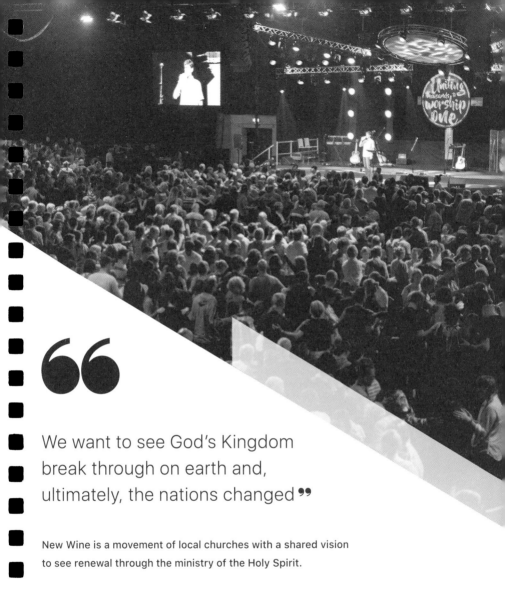

66

We want to see God's Kingdom
break through on earth and,
ultimately, the nations changed 99

**New Wine is a movement of local churches with a shared vision
to see renewal through the ministry of the Holy Spirit.**

Through training, mentoring and planting - delivered through local
churches and church leaders - we want to see God's Kingdom
break through on earth and, ultimately, the nations changed.